RONAY

A DESCRIPTION OF THE ISLANDS OF NORTH
RONA AND SULA SGEIR, TOGETHER WITH
THEIR GEOGRAPHY, TOPOGRAPHY,
HISTORY, AND NATURAL HISTORY,
ETC., TO WHICH IS APPENDED
A SHORT ACCOUNT OF THE
SEVEN HUNTERS, OR
FLANNAN ISLANDS

By

MALCOLM STEWART

OXFORD UNIVERSITY PRESS
LONDON: HUMPHREY MILFORD
1933

PRINTED IN GREAT BRITAIN

To the Memory of

DONALD MONRO
HIGH DEAN OF THE ISLES; *c.* 1550

MARTIN MARTIN
GENT; d. 1719

JOHN MacCULLOCH
M.D. 1773–1835

'O these endless little isles ! and
of all little isles this Ronay !
Yet, much as hath been seen, not to
see thee, lying clad with soft
verdure, and in thine awful solitude,
afar off in the lap of wild ocean,—
not to see thee with the carnal
eye, will be to have seen nothing !'

T. S. MUIR

RONAY

OXFORD
UNIVERSITY PRESS
AMEN HOUSE, E.C. 4
London Edinburgh Glasgow
Leipzig New York Toronto
Melbourne Capetown Bombay
Calcutta Madras Shanghai
HUMPHREY MILFORD
PUBLISHER TO THE
UNIVERSITY

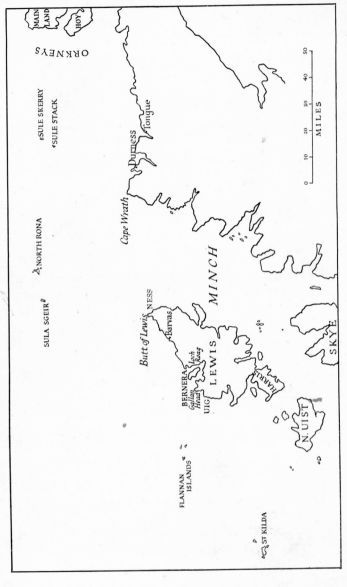

Fig. 1. MAP OF NORTH-WEST SCOTLAND

CONTENTS

LIST OF ILLUSTRATIONS

AUTHOR'S NOTE

THIS book was by no means written in a spirit of literary enthusiasm, but merely to set on record facts concerning these remote Western Isles. The author, remembering the great difficulties he experienced in tracing the history of these isles in old and obscure books and manuscripts, wishes merely to set down on paper the substance of these, together with his own impressions and experiences gained during a series of short visits to these islands.

One has heard much lately concerning St. Kilda and the evacuation of that island, but few seem to know that there are other Western Islands nearly as remote and much more desolate. Like St. Kilda, some of these have been inhabited; they too had their chapels and graveyards, but the people who faced the desolation of these isles have gone, and nothing remains but ruins, now the habitation of sea fowl. The islands are forgotten or unknown, and have even disappeared from the modern map of Scotland.

At the end of the description of each island the author has added a few short notes on the natural history. With the exception of Sula Sgeir, the fauna of the islands has been worked out at different times in very great detail. Since the scientific findings are largely the results of private and individual enterprise and research, and as many of the authors are still alive, the writer has in all fairness refrained from dealing with these in any detail, and after a brief outline has given the reference to the original papers, so that the reader may have no difficulty should he wish to study the natural history more closely.

There is a considerable amount of difference of opinion as to the spelling of the various place-names of these islands, and it is difficult to say which name is the more correct. The following are some of the various names given to the islands under review.

Ronay.	North Rona. (Ord. Survey)
Roney. (Harvie-Brown)	Rona.
Ronaidh. (Geol. map)	Ronaide. (Muir)
Sula Sgeir. (Ord. Survey)	North Barra.
Sulisker. (Admiralty Charts)	Barra.
Suiliskeray. (Monro)	
Sulisgeir. (Gurney & Harvie-Brown)	
Flannan Islands. (Ord. Survey)	Seven Hunters.
Flannen Islands.	Seven Haley Isles. (Monro)
Flannain Islands. (Muir)	Seaforth's Hunters.
Flanean Islands. (Blaeu's map, 1668)	Insulae Sacrae. (Buchanan)

With a view to establishing one name for each island, the names as given by the ordnance survey are suggested for adoption. Namely:

'North Rona', 'Sula Sgeir', and 'The Flannan Islands'.

The author wishes to express his gratitude to all those who have helped him in his work in the Isles. He particularly wishes to thank Mr. D. M. Reid, who was with him on North Rona in 1930, and Mr. T. H. Harrisson, who accompanied him to that island in the summer of the following year. On both these occasions the passage by steam trawler was granted by Mr. Mackie of Aberdeen. Sula Sgeir was also visited by steam trawler in the summer of 1932, thanks to the co-operation and help of Mr. Keir and Mr. Thompson of the Fishery Office, Aberdeen, and Captain Warman of Grimsby. Mr. J. Glencorse Wakelin, secretary to the Commissioners of Northern Lighthouses, gave much useful information, and he most kindly granted a passage on the *Pole Star* to Eilean Mor with the Flannan relief. A subsequent visit to the other Flannan Islands was made possible thanks to Mr. Malcolm MacLeod of Bernera.

The writer wishes to acknowledge his indebtedness to the following for permission to reproduce certain illustrations in this book:

Her Grace the Duchess of Bedford and Messrs. Oliver & Boyd Ltd. for the two photographs entitled 'Tunnel Cave, North Rona' and 'Looking South from Fianuis'; Mr. C. Dick Peddie and Mr. C. E. Cadger of the Northern Lighthouse Board for the two photographs 'Beannachadh, Eilean Mor' and 'Bothien Clann Igphail'; Messrs. Gurney & Jackson for the three photographs 'Eilean Mor from the South', 'Eilean Mor from the East', and 'The West Landing, Eilean Mor'. The maps of North Rona, Sula Sgeir, and the Flannan Islands were based, with permission, on publications of the Ordnance Survey. Finally, the five illustrations 'An Internal View of the East End of the Chapel', 'Ground Plan of Chapel, North Rona', 'An Old Cross', 'The Modern Tombstone', and 'Lighthouse, Eilean Mor' were drawn especially for this book by Mr. W. L. Roots, to whom the author expresses his grateful thanks.

NORTH RONA

Towards the top left-hand corner of the map the
county of Sutherland, as represented by a rather
crude yellow colouring, ends in Cape Wrath,
while an inch or so farther to the left the pink of the
Lewis terminates in the Butt. Between these two
there is nothing save a pale blue wash, the sea. To
the extreme north-east lie the Orkneys and Zetland,
with the little Fair Isle mid-distance between, but to
the north of the Cape and to the north of the Butt
the blue wash of the sea is uninterrupted.

The eleven miles tramp from the ferry is a long
one, but unavoidable since it is impossible to ferry
a car across the kyle. It is true that there is a car on
the far side belonging to the hotel at Keodale; no
one ever knows quite how it got there, but there it
is, and he is indeed a rich man who travels the road
on four wheels.

So the eleven miles on the rough track cut through
the peat moss is unavoidable. But who would want
to miss a road so wonderful? Occasionally the
traveller reaches a viewpoint or rise in the road and
pauses to look back to trace the meandering Dionard
entering the picture from behind the foot of rugged
Foinaven. He looks forward too and sees the track
winding down before him for the next three to four
miles. With face set he continues once more on his
way and at length reaches the lighthouse.

From the high tower of the light the whole world
seems to open at his feet. To the south, past the

rugged cliffs of the Cape, he sees the little isle of Am Balg by Sandwood, that arm of the sea long since silted up to form an inland loch, and beyond to Rhu Stoer; to the east, Fharaid and the limestone cliffs of Whiten, while beyond he gazes on the massive three-fold peak of Loyal and the cone of Hope. But to the north he knows there is nothing save the sea, the great expanse of the North Atlantic. And while he looks he discerns a speck on the horizon. Some ship, maybe from a Scandinavian port, that has travelled through the Pentland westward bound. But no, that cannot be, for the object is stationary. What is it then? For all the accuracy of the map can this be land?

The *Sophos* had pitched and rolled much on her journey north from Aberdeen, but the sea calmed considerably as the trawler raced through the Pentland with the ebbing tide. In fact it seemed to take hardly any time to steam along the northern coasts of Caithness and Sutherland. The sun was sinking in the summer night, and as the ship steamed by, towering precipitous cliffs blue in the evening light gave way to the great sea lochs. Here was something that the very fjords of Norway could never rival. But all too soon the land ended in the lighthouse which was ever sending forth its red flashes to warn navigation that here was the north-west extremity of the mainland, and here the hard cruel cliffs of gneiss that had resisted the lashing waves of the ocean since time before the Himalayas were beneath the seas. The telegraph rang and a new course was set north-

Photo.   *M.S.*

FIG. 2. NORTH RONA FROM THE EAST

Photo.   *M.S.*

FIG. 3. THE S.W. EXTREMITY FROM THE VILLAGE

north-west, and gradually as the trawler steamed into the night the red light of Cape Wrath was left behind.

With the cold grey light of breaking dawn land was clearly discernible some few miles off the starboard bow. The log read forty miles. As the ship approached, so the land grew and grew until it was easily possible to make out the shape of the island. The southern half was steep and precipitous, the cliffs towering out of the sea; thin tops green with luxuriant vegetation. The Atlantic swell beat untiringly and mercilessly at their feet. The north, however, was much lower and appeared in contrast to the south to be little more than a reef of rock, a skerry uplifted from the ocean floor.

A boat was lowered. Though so easily said, this operation required many minutes to perform, since it had not been lowered in many years, a point of honour amongst trawlermen. The best place for getting ashore appeared to be in a small inlet towards the centre of the east side. But even here landing was by no means easy, for the swell lifted and lowered the small boat ceaselessly. A quick jump ashore while the boat rose and a desperate grab at the rock was the only possible course to adopt, while the gear had to be thrown ashore piecemeal. This too was hard, since some of the cases were heavy—two men cannot live five days on an island without food and clothing as a protection against the cold nights.

As the trawler steamed on its way two men were left over forty miles from the nearest soul, with a great expanse of sea between, but with an unknown island at their feet to explore.

To quote Capt. Burnaby, 'the island has the shape of a decanter with the neck towards the north'. This description is fairly accurate, North Rona having a maximum length of one mile north and south, while a similar breadth east and west occurs towards the south of the island. The central part of the island forms a high ridge which stretches from Ton Breighe in the west to Sron nam Caorach in the east, the highest point of 355 feet being attained near the east end. From this hill-ridge the ground slopes gradually in a south-west direction, the lowest part being the barren rock ridge of Sceapull, the south-west extremity. To the north of the central hill-ridge the ground falls very rapidly to the 'neck of the decanter' which commences at Sgeildige, the famous tunnel cave, and Geodha Stoth. The northern extremity of the island Fianuis (witness) is flat and almost unfertile. As shown by the photographs there is a remarkable similarity of appearance between these north and south-west extremities. North Rona, whose total area comprises some 300 acres, is completely cliff bound, and nowhere is there to be found any beach or shore. The cliffs are sheer and of great height; occasional ledges in them, however, form the habitat of milliards of sea fowl. Such is the continual force of the Atlantic to which the island is subjected, that on all sides the sea has eroded the cliffs to form caves and 'geos'. Poll Thothatom is a very good example of a geo,

Photo. M.S.

FIG. 4. THE CENTRAL HILL-RIDGE OF RONA

Photo. M.S.

FIG. 5. LEAC NA SGROB

while the tunnel cave of Sgeildige is now well known. The entrance to this cave is a rounded arch fifty feet in height, while the cave itself is about a hundred feet long, extending half-way through the narrow neck of land. The remarkable feature of this cave lies in a small natural shaft that runs from the top, a few yards north of the cave, and enters into the end of the cave just above sea-level. The entrance to this shaft is a hole 3 ft. 6 in. high and 9 ft. broad.

The water round North Rona is deep, and there are few obstructions to navigation. There are two rocks, Harsgeir and Loba Sgeir, off the south-west end, and another off the north end, but these are only separated from the main part of the island by a few yards. However, there is a larger skerry, Gealldruig Mhor, a third of a mile south of the south-east end, with a small sunken rock between. Another sunken rock lies some 300 yards east of Loba Sgeir.

Landing on the island is at all times difficult, and only possible in the very finest of weather. The best places are Geodha Stoth in the east and Stoc a Phriosain in the south. The former is usually the easier as the cliffs here are very low, but it is a considerable distance to carry gear from here up the hill and down towards the ruined village. On the other hand, Stoc a Phriosain is directly below the ruins, but there is a considerable cliff to climb before the summit is attained. Should both these places be found impracticable owing to the wind, Marcasgeo on the south-west may be attempted, though it is inclined to be dangerous owing to swell and sunken rocks.

With the exception of the extreme north and south-west points the island has luxuriant vegetation, the grass in places being of remarkable height. This forms good pasturage for sheep. There is no running water on North Rona, but since there is never any shortage of rain, water may be obtained by digging about the south of the village. The water is only seepage, but moderately clear and fresh; care, however, must be taken to keep it free from pollution by the birds. Wells were made (in a similar way) by the former inhabitants. These measure about two to three feet square and are flagged and covered with stone. Though several are marked on the map, only one, namely that near Poll Heallair, is at present of any use.

Of the ruins of the houses, the chapel, the cairns, piles, walls, and the relics of previous habitation, more will be said later.

First impressions are always most important, for they are present in the mind when one looks back on places visited in the past. No one could ever fail to experience immense pleasure on first landing on North Rona. A narrow strip of land, on the north end covered with green vegetation and surrounded on three sides by the ever-present Atlantic. To the south the island rises sharply to the central hill-ridge, beyond which is dead ground, lost to the eye of the observer. The natural stillness and the solitude of the place are broken by the cries of sea fowl, and the beat of the waves. You may be alone here on North Rona, but for all that the island is teeming with other

Photo. *Duchess of Bedford.*

FIG. 6. TUNNEL CAVE, NORTH RONA

Photo. *Duchess of Bedford.*

FIG. 7. LOOKING SOUTH FROM FIANUIS

animal life. Two hundred sheep, and milliards of gulls, not to mention the seals that are ever habitants of North Rona. Well they know the beauties of the place, but few let out their secret to the poor human.

The climb towards the south is steep, especially when encumbered by stores and baggage. The steep slope up from the north end to the centre of the island is a feature never exhibited on the map, but by those who have climbed it, it must always be remembered. Once the arduous task is done, and the summit of the ridge is reached, one may once more look down and see the ocean to the south. To the south-east lies the highest point of the island. Though this point seems to have no official name, Muir called it Aonach-Comh-Dheuchainne. To the east is a small white conical hill, much resembling a pyramid of ancient Egypt, but to the south-west the land is still hidden. Here one walks through the long grass and, as the ground slopes away before one, comes suddenly upon the village encircled by its wall.

Ruins of villages deserted for many a year usually induce a feeling of despondency and regret, not to mention solitude, but here, however, though one stands and ponders upon the men who lived here before, one has no such thoughts of sadness. So old are the buildings and so unique their construction, that now they are entirely overgrown with turf, and only being a few feet above the surface are almost indistinguishable from the surrounding ground.

The houses are probably four or five in number, but owing to their state of collapse it is somewhat hard to be certain. They are, of course, all 'dry stone' built. Slabs of rock probably collected from Sceapull, the south-west extremity of the island, often many hundredweight in size, are placed one upon the other. The men who constructed these buildings well knew their art, for nowhere do buildings of cemented stone and like material stand up to the elements like these dry stone buildings of the Isles. The architects too were ingenious. Here is a place some forty miles out in the open Atlantic exposed to the full force of the gale. How best can buildings be constructed to stand against such odds?

The building of the houses half underground has done much to protect them. Three feet of wall above and three below the ground is how these buildings were constructed, and it is significant that all the doors face eastwards, the prevailing wind coming from the south-west. This underground building was carried to such perfection that MacCulloch recording his own visit writes:

'Such is the violence of the wind in this region that not even the solid mass of a highland house can resist it. The house is therefore excavated in the earth, the wall required for the support of the roof scarcely rising two feet above the surface. The roof itself is but little raised above the level, and is covered with a great weight of turf, above which is the thatch; the whole being surrounded with turf stacks to ward off the gales. The entrance to this sub-terranean retreat is through a long, dark, narrow, and tortuous passage like the gallery of a mine, commencing by an aperture not three feet high and

FIG. 8. FIANUIS

FIG. 9. FIANUIS

very difficult to find. With little trouble it might be effectually concealed; nor, were the fire suppressed, could the existence of a house be suspected, the whole having the appearance of a collection of turf stacks and dunghills. Although our conference had lasted some time, none of the party discovered that it was held on the roof of the house. . . . The interior strongly resembles that of a Kamschatkan hut; receiving no other light than that from the smoke hole, being covered with ashes, festooned with strings of dried fish, filled with smoke, and having scarcely an article of furniture. Such is life in North Rona . . .'

The houses were by no means all similar in design; one of those served by a passage is of incredible size, measuring some fifteen to thirty feet in length. This house is complete with hearth, but goodness knows what the inhabitants ever found to burn on it. By far the most superior and almost certainly latest house stands by itself a few yards west of the chapel. It is in a state of remarkable preservation. Internally it is 16 ft. 10 in. long, by 9 ft. 3 in. wide at the west end and 8 ft. 9 in. at the east end. It has a height measured from the floor to the bottom of the sloping roof of 5 ft. 11 in. In the east end there is a small window 5 ft. high, 3 ft. 7 in. broad at the bottom, and 3 ft. broad at the top. There is also a door in this wall 4 ft. 9 in. high, 2 ft. 9 in. wide at the bottom, and 2 ft. 6 in. at the top. Externally the overall length of the house is 24 ft. with a maximum width of 15 ft. The height of the gable from the floor is 8 ft. 9 in., while the chimney adds another foot on to this

measurement. Externally the window is only 4 ft.
7 in. high and 2 ft. 3 in. wide. The thickness of this
wall varies from 2 ft. 6 in. to 2 ft. 9 in. Outside the
doorway there is a small courtyard some 12 ft.
square. These measurements give some idea of the
size of the building. It is very solidly built, being
practically entirely underground and completely
sheltered. This house had obviously a sloping roof,
but since at the present time none of the houses has
retained its roof, it is difficult to speculate as to its
nature. They were, however, almost certainly constructed of stone flags of great size gradually built
inwards to cover the whole of the roof. This building was in all probability the manse.

By far the most famous and interesting of the
buildings on North Rona is the chapel. This chapel
is now deteriorating rapidly, and though recom-
mended by the Royal Commission on Ancient and
Historical Monuments to be cared for, little or
nothing has yet been done. It would be absolutely
unforgivable if this unique building was permitted
to become a total ruin. The chapel consists clearly
of two portions; an eastern and older part, and a
western and more recent part. There is no better
description of this chapel than that of Muir, who
studied it in very great detail at a time when it was
more complete than it is now.

'Of Teampull Rona', remarks Muir, 'on the outside it is for the most part a rounded heap of stones
roofed over with turf. Within you find it a roughly
built cell, 9 ft. 3 in. in height, and at the floor 11 ft.
6 in. long and 7 ft. 6 in. wide. The end walls lean

Photo. *M.S.*

FIG. 10. THE MANSE, NORTH RONA

Photo. *M.S.*

FIG. 11. THE CHAPEL, WEST END

inwards a little, the side ones so greatly that, where they meet the flat slab forming their roof, they are scarcely two feet apart. Beyond the singularity of its shape, there is nothing remarkable in the building, its only minute features being a square doorway in the west end, so low that you have to creep on your elbows and knees, and a flat-headed window, without splay on either side 19 in. long and 8 in. wide set over the doorway; another window of like form and length but an inch or two wider is placed near the east end of the south wall. .... Attached as a nave to the west end of the cell and externally co-extensive with it in breadth are the remains of another chapel, internally 14 ft. 8 in. in length and 8 ft. 3 in. in width'.

Unlike any other building on the island the east end of the chapel has been roughly lime cemented at some date subsequent to its foundation. This chapel, which Muir claims to be eighth or ninth century, is complete with the exception of a small portion knocked away from the east end. The west end is at least some one to two hundred years subsequent to the east end. Very little of this newer part now remains, except for the wall, some ten feet of which still stand at the extreme west end. This building, which was constructed wholly above the ground, must have been by far the largest on the whole island.

No church or chapel is complete without its graveyard, and on North Rona this is situated to the north of the chapel, and enclosed by a low wall with a doorway on the south-west. Here are several

FIG. 12. AN INTERNAL VIEW OF THE EAST END OF THE
CHAPEL

(W. L. ROOTS *after* T. S. MUIR)

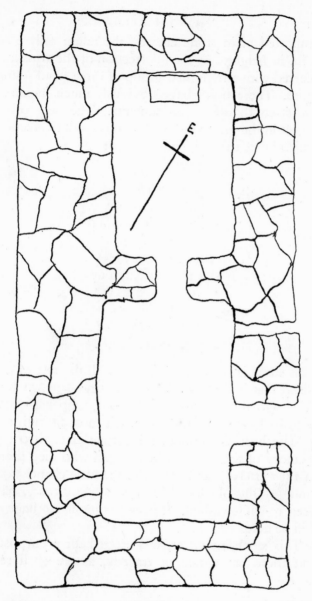

FIG. 13. GROUND PLAN OF CHAPEL, NORTH RONA

(W. L. ROOTS *after* T. S. MUIR)

truncated plain stone crosses, the tallest only 2 ft. 6 in. in height. At the intersection of the arms it is pierced with a triangular group of three small round holes. These holes have obviously much impaired the strength of the monuments. The only other object in the graveyard is a hideous modern erection which bears the following legend:

SACRED

TO

THE MEMORY OF

MALCOLM M'C DONALD

NESS

WHO DIED AT RONA

FEB 18 1885 AGED 67

ALSO M M'C KAY

WHO DIED AT RONA SAME TIME

'Blessed are the dead
who die in the Lord'.

This stone is so out of keeping with the rest of the island that it is a real blot on the landscape. A few years ago the Duchess of Bedford, who has often been to North Rona, described it most fittingly:

'The horrible modern tombstone erected to the memory of the last two inhabitants who died there in 1887 (1885?), and placed in the little chapel yard amongst the old locally carved stone crosses, had been re-whitewashed. If ever I commit sacrilege it will be here.'

This stone, however, was erected for a purpose, and there lies a tale of tragedy, as we shall see later.

This little isle standing by itself far off in the open Atlantic, its ruined houses, its unique chapel, its deserted dead; surely these must have some tale to tell. What has become of its people? What misfortune overtook the island that now nothing but ruins remain, the inhabitants dead and forgotten, and the island unknown?

Serious thought and spiritual occupation of the mind necessitate quiet and seclusion. But as is always the case, the petty quarrelling and scolding of women folk is inconsistent with such meditation. Such was the state of affairs in Eorrapidh.

The saintly man living quietly in Teampull Rona near the Butt of the Lewis was for ever disturbed by the ceaseless babble of the female tongue. What wonder then that he turned to find somewhere more suitable for his rest and repose. So being a man of prayer he turned to God with his tale of woe, and in a vision was told to go to the beach on the morrow.

The advantage of being a saintly and god-fearing man appears to be that when in difficulties the whole of the animal kingdom will come to one's aid. And here was no exception, for on the morrow there appeared a whale a small distance from the shore, and like another of these holy men, he mounted on her back and was taken off across the wild ocean. After days of such ocean-travel this Jonah landed on a little island appropriately called Ronay on account of its seal inhabitants, and from this island the saint derived his name.

But even here the saint was not at peace, for he

FIG. 14. AN OLD CROSS

(W. L. ROOTS *after* T. S. MUIR)

FIG. 15.   THE MODERN TOMBSTONE
(W. L. ROOTS)

D

found the island in possession of the devil. The devil always appears under a number of guises, and on Rona this guise was by no means the least unattractive. Here he assumed the form of a mob of monstrous hairy animals resembling dogs, with long claws and great round red eyes glowing like hot coals. As is nearly always the case in these disputes between saint and devil, good prevails, and at length these beasts were driven off the island backward before the advance of St. Ronan. As these beasts disappeared over the edge of the cliff they made one last desperate effort to obtain a hold, but in vain, and as they slipped into the sea they scratched the rock with their claws. This place of their somewhat hurried departure is called Leac na Sgrob, the scratched declivity, and the scratches on the rocks are to be seen to this day.

While one does not like to disbelieve this delightful story, there is also an equally plausible geological explanation for these 'scratches'.

Wishing for somewhere to live, St. Ronan now set to work and built the original and east end of the present chapel. But even then the saint was not freed from evil influences, for did not the devil cause the winds to blow and the sea to beat upon the island? So strong were these elements of nature that the saint feared for his chapel, for one of the walls was as yet not too strong. However, being evidently a man of resource, he leant against this wall upon the inside, and for all the wind and weather the devil could do no more than bend it.

All this is said to have taken place in the eighth

or ninth century, and little else is known with certainty (!) concerning these early years.

The west end of the chapel is supposed to have been built some one or two centuries later, while another chapel, the site of which is now unknown, was built by the Roman Catholics a few yards east of the present chapel. This building, which was roofed with wood and thatched with straw, was called Teampull nam Manach, and was about the same size as the western part of the present chapel. This chapel was pulled down about the year 1250, but at the beginning of the nineteenth century some three feet of wall were still standing. Now it is absolutely impossible to find any trace of such a building.

So much for mythology, parts of it true, no doubt, the tales being handed down by word of mouth throughout the generations. The first authentic account of the island is that of Donald Monro, High Dean of the Isles, who toured the Hebrides in the early year of 1594. His account, though interesting, is short, and the Dean's estimates of distance were by no means always accurate.

Our early knowledge of North Rona is due entirely to Martin Martin whose *Description of the Western Islands* was published in 1716. We gather that most of Martin's information was obtained from Daniel Morison, minister of Barvas, after his return from Rona which then belonged to him as part of his glebe. Of such importance is this account of Martin that it is here given in full.

'The island Rona is reckoned about 20 leagues from the north-east point of Ness in Lewis, and counted but a mile in length, and about half a mile in breadth: it hath a hill in the west part, and is only visible from the Lewis in a fair summers-day. I had an account of this island, and the custom of it from several natives of Lewis, who had been to the place; but more particularly from Mr. Daniel Morison, minister of Barvas, after his return from Rona island, which then belonged to him as part of his glebe. Upon my landing (says he) the natives received me very affectionately, and addressed me with their usual salutation to a stranger: "God save you pilgrim, you are heartily welcome here; for we have had repeated apparitions of your person among us (after the manner of second sight) and we heartily congratulate your arrival in this our remote country." One of the natives would needs express his high esteem for my person, by making a turn round about me sun-ways, and at the same time blessing me, and wishing me all happiness; but I bid him let alone that piece of homage, telling him I was sensible to his good meaning towards me; but this poor man was not little disappointed, as were also his neighbours; for they doubted not that this ancient ceremony would have been very acceptable to me: and one of them told me, that this was a thing due to my character from them, as to their chief and patron, and they could not, nor would not, fail to perform it. They conducted me to the little village where they dwell, and in the way thither there were three enclosures; and as I entered each of these, the inhabitants severally saluted me, taking me by the hand, and saying, "Traveller, you are welcome here".

They went along with me to the house that they had assigned for my lodging; where there was a bundle of straw laid on the floor, for a seat for me to sit on. After a little time was spent in general discourse, the inhabitants retired to their respective dwelling-houses; and in this interval, they killed each man a sheep, being in all five, answerable to the number of their families. The skins of the sheep were entire, and flayed off so from the neck to the tail, that they were in form like a sack. These skins being flayed off after this manner, were by the inhabitants instantly filled with barley-meal; and this they gave me by way of a present: one of their number acted as speaker for the rest, saying, "Traveller, we are very sensible of the favour you have done us in coming so far with a design to instruct us in our way to happiness, and at the same time to venture yourself on the great ocean; pray be pleased to accept this small present, which we humbly offer as an expression of our sincere love to you". This I accepted, though in a very coarse dress; but it was given with such an air of hospitality and goodwill, as deserved thanks. They presented my man also with some pecks of meal, as being likewise a traveller: the boat's-crew having been in Rona before, were not reckoned strangers, and therefore there was no present given them, but their daily maintenance.

'There is a chapel here dedicated to St. Ronan, fenced with a stone-wall round it; and they take care to keep it neat and clean, and sweep it every day. There is an altar in it, on which there lies a big plank of wood about ten feet in length; every foot has a hole in it, and in every hole a stone, to which the natives ascribe several virtues: one of them is singular, as they say, for promoting speedy delivery to a woman in travail.

'They repeat the Lord's Prayer, Creed, and Ten Commandments in the chapel every Sunday morning. They have cows, sheep, barley, and oats, and live a harmless life, being perfectly ignorant of most of those vices that abound in the world. They know nothing of money or gold having no occasion for either; they neither buy nor sell, but only barter for such little things as they want: they covet no wealth, being fully content and satisfied with food and raiment; though at the same time they are very precise in the matter of property among themselves; for none of them will by any means allow his neighbour to fish within his property; and every one must exactly observe not to make any incroachment on his neighbour. They have an agreeable and hospitable temper for all strangers: they concern not themselves about the rest of mankind, except the inhabitants in the north part of Lewis. They take their surname from the colour of the sky, rainbow, and clouds. There are only five families in this small island, and every tenant hath his dwelling-house, a barn, a house where their best effects are preserved, a house for their cattle, and a porch on each side of the door to keep off the rain and snow. Their houses are built with stone and thatched with straw, which is kept down with ropes of the same, poised with stones. They wear the same habit with those in

Lewis, and speak only Irish. When any of them comes to the Lewis, which is seldom, they are astonished to see so many people. They much admire greyhounds and love to have their company. They are mightily pleased at the sight of horses; and one of them observing a horse to neigh, asked if the horse laughed at him. A boy from Rona perceiving a colt running towards him, was so much frighted at it, that he jumped into a bush of nettles, where his whole skin became full of blisters.

'Another of the natives of Rona having had the opportunity of travelling as far as Coul, in the Shire of Ross, which is the seat of Sir Alexander Mac-Kenzie, everything he saw was surprising to him; and when he heard the noise of those who walked in the rooms above him, he presently fell to the ground, thinking thereby to save his life, for he supposed that the house was coming down over his head. When Mr. Morison the minister was in Rona, two of the natives courted a maid with intention to marry her; and being married to one of them afterwards, the other was not a little disappointed, because there was no other match for him in this island. The wind blowing fair, Mr. Morison sailed directly for Lewis; but after three hours sailing was forced back to Rona by a contrary wind: and at his landing the poor man that had lost his sweetheart was overjoyed, and expressed himself in these words, "I bless God and Ronan that you are returned again, for I hope you will now make me happy, and give me a right to enjoy the woman every other year by turns, that so both may have issue by her". Mr. Morison could not refrain from smiling at this unexpected request, chid the man for his unreasonable demand, and desired him to have patience for a year longer, and he would send him a wife from Lewis; but this did not ease the poor man who was tormented with the thought of dying without issue.

'Another who wanted a wife, and having got a shilling from a seaman that happened to land there, went and gave this shilling to Mr. Morison, to purchase him a wife in Lewis, and send her to him, for he was told that this piece of money was a thing of extraordinary value; and his desire was gratified the ensuing year.

'About 14 years ago a swarm of rats, but none knows how, came into Rona, and in a short time eat up all the corn in the island. In a few months after, some seamen landed there, who robbed the poor people of their bull. These misfortunes and the want of supply from Lewis for the space of a year, occasioned the death of all that ancient race of people. The steward of St. Kilda being by a storm driven there told me that he found a woman with her child on her breast, both lying dead at the side of a rock. Some years after, the minister (to whom the island belongeth) sent a new colony to this island with suitable supplies. The following year a boat was sent to them with some more supplies, and orders to receive the rents; but the boat being lost as it is supposed, I can give no further account of this late plantation.

'The inhabitants of this little island say that the cuckow is never seen or heard here, but after the death of the Earl of Seaforth, or the minister.'

About the same time was published *An Account of Hirta and Rona*, given to Sir Robert Sibbald by the Lord Register, Sir George M'Kenzie of Tarbat. An interesting point in this account is the fact that at this time 'Rona had for many generations been inhabited by five families, which seldom exceeded thirty souls in all; they had a kind of commonwealth among them, in so far if any of them have more children than another, he that had fewer took from the other what his number equalled, and the excrescence of above thirty souls was taken with the summer boat to the Lewis to the Earl of Seaforth, their master, to whom they paid yearly some quantity of meal stitched up in sheep's skins, and feather of sea fowls.

'They have no fuel for fire upon the island; but by the special providence of God, the sea yearly casts in so much timber as serves them: their sheep there have wool, but of a bluish colour.

'There is a chapel in the midst of the isle, where they meet twice or thrice a day. One of the families is hereditary beddal, and the master of that stands at the altar and prayeth, the rest kneel upon their knees and join with him. Their religion is the Romish religion: there is always one who is the chief, and commands the rest, and they are so well satisfied with their condition that they exceedingly bewail the condition of those, as supernumerary, they must send out of the island.'

The next account of North Rona is by MacCulloch. 'Years had passed in vain attempts, and still we had not reached North Rona', thus writes the 'stone

E

doctor' in the commencement of his description of this island, the result of a visit in the early nineteenth century. His description, though occupying many pages, has really little substance in it. He had much to say about the wrong determination of the latitude and longitude, but for all that, he himself nearly doubled the height of the eastern hill.

At this time visits to the island were obviously very few and far between, for we learn that on his arrival the men and women ran away and hid. This is hardly surprising, since except for the occasional visit of boats from the *Fortunée* engaged in cruising after the president in 1812, and the twice yearly visits of the boat collecting rents, the inhabitants had seen no one.

For services rendered, Kenneth MacCragie received food for himself and his family, and two pounds paid in clothes, which had to robe some six individuals. He had, too, a cow brought from Lewis when in milk and exchanged when unserviceable. From the milk of his sheep he contrived to make cheeses, some of which the doctor took away with him. The cottar, so we learn, was bound to the island for eight years, and was not even allowed a boat since it would only offer the poor man a temptation to drown himself.

'The soil', writes MacCulloch, 'is of good quality, and produces barley, oats, and potatoes. The average surplus of corn remaining beyond the consumption of the family was stated at eight bolls of barley; and this, united to the produce of the sheep, and an annual supply of eight stone of feathers, is, to the tenant, the value of North Rona. To him, who is one of the tacksmen of Lewis, the land is let for two pound a year.

'There is no other water in the island than that which is collected in pools from the rain, but there is no chance of any deficiency in this article. As there is no peat, turf is used for fuel and the oil of the cuddy for light; but, with characteristic improvidence, there are no means of lighting the fire should it ever be extinguished. Well may the vestals of their cottage watch the smoky embers and trim the dying lamp.'

Little more is known of the inhabitants of this Atlantic outpost. The last family upon Rona was that of a shepherd named Donald M'Leod, otherwise the king of Rona, who returned to the Lewis in 1844, since when it has been uninhabited except for a few days at the annual sheep-shearing at the end of July.

Shortly after the evacuation we learn that the island was offered gratis by Sir James Matheson to the government as a penal settlement, but that the offer was refused.

All further accounts of the island were, alas, written by men who visited it subsequent to the evacuation. T. S. Muir, who was there in 1857, and again three years later, took with him a youth, a former islander, and through Muir's work much has been learned concerning the local superstitions. His plans and measurements of the chapel are very accurate, while details now no longer visible were all recorded by his pen. Subsequent visits to the island are unilluminating as regards the life of the former inhabitants, and all the relatively numerous landings that were made at the close of the last century and the commencement of the present are of little significance save from a purely scientific aspect.

However, one cannot pass on without mentioning a tragedy that occurred on the island in 1885. Harvie-Brown, who visited the island later in that year, has gathered the main facts of the case, and nothing can be better than to set down his actual words.

'The names of the two men who went from Lewis to Roney were Murdoch Mackay and Malcolm MacDonald, two good representatives of the Danish and Celtic types. Having objections to the appointment of a layman as preacher to the church at Ness, and being grieved at some feeling shown them in consequence of the action which they took along with a few others of the congregation, they were desirous of making some atonement for their opposition, and resolved to leave the place.

'Accordingly, on the morning of Monday, 20th May 1884, they sailed for the island of North Roney, where they landed that night. Ostensibly their reason for going there was to take care of the sheep on the island, but in reality it was to atone for their action against the minister that they went into exile. Twice did boats go out to North Roney—in the following August and September—and the friends endeavoured to get the two men to return to their families and friends, but in vain. The men were then in good health, and apparently enjoyed their island home, and employed themselves in building sheep

fanks, fishing, and killing seals. It was only, however, on the 22nd April 1885, after two previous
unsuccessful attempts, that they effected a landing.
No one met them. At the door of the little half-
underground house occupied by the two men the
boatmen found the body of Malcolm MacDonald in
a sitting position beside an improvised fireplace, as
if he had fallen asleep. On the floor of the house,
beside the fireplace, lay the body of Murdoch
Mackay. His tartan plaid was placed neatly and care-
fully over and under him, showing that the deft
hands and warm heart of Malcolm MacDonald had
performed the last sad office to the body of his dead
friend. The bodies were wrapped in canvas wrap-
pings, and buried side by side in the primitive and
beautifully situated burial-place adjoining.

'It was feared that the poor men might have met
with foul play, and the matter having been brought
up in Parliament, the Crown authorities ordered an
investigation. Accordingly, the procurator-fiscal,
Stornoway, and two medical men, proceeded to
Roney in the fishing cutter *Vigilant*. The bodies of
the two men were exhumed, and a post-mortem
examination made. There was no appearance of foul
play; it was ascertained that Murdoch Mackay died
of acute inflammation of the right lung and left
kidney, and that Malcolm MacDonald died from
cold, exposure, and exhaustion. The opinion among
the friends is that Malcolm MacDonald assiduously
attended his friend day and night till he died, by
which time he himself became so weak that he could
not bury the body, and being unable to remain in the

hut had sat down by the improvised fire and died. There was a small pot on the little fireplace at the door, indicating that Malcolm MacDonald meant to prepare for himself some food, which, however, he was never destined to eat. The medical examiners found nothing in his stomach but a few grains of meal and a little brown liquid—probably tea. An abundance of unconsumed food was found in the hut. On this occasion the son of Malcolm MacDonald took two coffins with him to Roney, and the two friends were re-interred again side by side as before.

'The men would seem to have spent their time in prayer and meditation, and in reading the Gaelic Scriptures, in which they were well versed. Neither of them could write, but they kept a record of their time—of the days, weeks, and the months—in a very ingenious manner. This was accomplished by means of a bar of red pine wood, evenly and accurately dressed, 2 feet long and $1\frac{1}{8}$ inches in the side. A notch is neatly cut in the corner of the bar for each day of the week, and then a deeper notch for Sunday, while for the end of the month a cut is made from side to side of the bar. The plan is simple, clever, and intelligible. The markings begin on Friday, the 21st June, 1884, and cease on Tuesday the 17th February 1885. Towards the end the notches are less neatly and accurately made, indicating very clearly that the deft fingers which fashioned the rest were becoming weak and powerless to cut into the hard pine wood. These notches are no less touching than instructive, and speak to the eye and to the heart and the imagination with a pathos all their own. Through a hole in the end of the calendar is a looped cord by which to suspend the stick.'

When the Great War shook the whole world, it is interesting to note that the little island of North Rona was not overlooked, for we learn that 'On the 23rd August the *Sappho* was sent to search N. Rona island, a statement having been received indicating that it might possibly have been used by the enemy as a base for aircraft. She reported, after examination, that the island was, as expected, unsuitable for such a purpose' (!)

North Rona, together with Sula Sgeir, form part of the parish of Barvas in Lewis, and at the present time are rented by Mr. Alexander MacFarquhar of Dell, Ness.

And now the island is desolate, and once more the island of perpetual mist, as the stone doctor termed it. The waves of the wild Atlantic for ever beat on its lonely shore, and few there be that now land to climb the eastern hill, and see on a summer's day the far-off hills stretching from the Hoy to the Lewis. The people are gone, a race is lost, there is no one left to grind the meal in the old stone querns. The chapel once kept swept and cleaned is now the nesting-place of the fulmar. There is none to look through the holes of the crosses at the altar candles on New Year's eve, and none to hand on the legend of their patron, the godly Ronan. Only the ruins stand as a memorial to a lost people, and again the island is left to its bird life while the seals sport in the caves. The unwatched sheep roam the green and fertile hills, once cultivated by man, till the following summer when they are exchanged for others from the Lewis.

NATURAL HISTORY

North Rona is happily entirely devoid of vermin. There are no rabbits, lizards, toads, or frogs on the island, while extensive trapping by the Duchess of Bedford, Mr. T. H. Harrisson, and the author has failed to secure any mice or rats.

The largest mammal is the grey seal, *Halichoerus grypus*, which breeds on the low rocky parts of the shore and on the neighbouring skerries. Mr. T. H. Harrisson has estimated their number at 250, but this is almost certainly on the high side. About 200 sheep, belonging to Mr. MacFarquhar of Ness, are left on the island on account of the good pasturage. They are exchanged annually for others from the Lewis.

In common with all the remote western skerries, North Rona possesses a unique and very extensive collection of birds. The most important among them is, of course, the Leach's Fork Tail Petrel, *Oceanodroma leucorrhoa leucorrhoa*. In Scotland, this small petrel only breeds here, on St. Kilda, the Flannan Islands, and probably on Sula Sgeir. On North Rona it burrows in the turf in the ruined walls of the village, and during the summer it is purely nocturnal. On a moonlight night, while the seals are for ever barking, it is a delightful sight to watch these small birds flying down the wind into the night. They have a very peculiar call, and night on North

Rona is considerably more noisy than day. These petrels possess a very erratic flight, and a head-on collision between two has been observed, both birds having fallen to the ground after the impact. Since these birds live in the walls of the ruins, it is by no means always pleasant to sleep in one of the houses. A petrel perched on one's nose is not necessarily always pleasant.

Another bird very common on Rona is the fulmar, *Fulmarus glacialis glacialis*, which breeds here on the top of the island in the open. This bird when young makes excellent eating, though inclined to be of an oily nature. John Morisone makes some very interesting observations as to the various uses to which this bird was put.

'There are also, 17 leagues from the Lews and to the north of it, the islands called Suliskerr which is the westmost, and Ronay fyve miles to the eas(t) of it; Ronay (onlie) inhabited and ordinarlie be five small tennents. Their ordinar is to have all things common: they have a considerable grouth of victual (onlie bear). The best of their sustinance is fowl, which they take in girns and sometimes in a stormie night they creep to them where they sleep thickest, and throwing some handfulls of sand over their heads as if it were hailes, they take them be the necks. Of the grease of those fowls (especiallie the Solind Goose) they make an excellent oyle called gibanir-tick, which is exceeding good for healing of anie sore ore wound ore cancer, either man or beast. This myself found true by experience by applying it to the legg of a young gentleman which had been

F

inflamed and cankered for the space of two years,
and his father being a trader south and north, sought
all phisicians and doctors with whom he had occasion to meet; but all was in vain. Yet in two weeks
time, being in my hous, was perfetlie whole be
applying the forsaid oyle. The way they make it
is,—they put the grease and fatt into the great gutt
of the fowll and so it is hung within a hous untill
it run in oyle. In this Ronay are two little cheapels
where sanct Ronan lived all his tyme as an hermit.'

The following is a list of the resident and migratory birds of North Rona as given by Mr. T. H.
Harrisson:

Corvus cornix cornix. Hooded crow.
Sturnus vulgaris vulgaris. Starling.
Loxia curvirostra curvirostra. Crossbill.
Passer montanus. Tree-sparrow.
Motacilla flava rayi. Yellow wagtail.
Motacilla alba yarrelli. White wagtail.
Motacilla alba alba. Pied wagtail.
Anthus trivialis trivialis. Tree-pipit.
Anthus pratensis. Meadow-pipit.
Anthus spinoletta petrosus. Rock-pipit.
Muscicapa hypoleuca hypoleuca. Pied flycatcher.
Phylloscopus collybita collybita. Chiffchaff.
Phylloscopus trochilus trochilus. Willow-warbler.
Sylvia nisoria nisoria. Barred warbler.
Sylvia curruca curruca. Lesser whitethroat.
Turdus philomelos? subsp. Song-thrush.
Œnanthe œnanthe œnanthe. Common wheatear.
Œnanthe œnanthe leucorrhoa. Greenland wheat-
ear.

Saxicola rubetra rubetra. Whinchat.

Hirundo rustica rustica. Swallow.

Delichon urbica urbica. House-martin.

Falco peregrinus peregrinus. Peregrine falcon.

Circus cyaneus cyaneus. Hen-harrier.

Ardea cinerea cinerea. Heron.

Somateria mollissima mollissima. Eider.

Mergus serrator. Red-breasted merganser.

Phalacrocorax carbo carbo. Cormorant.

Phalacrocorax graculus graculus. Shag.

Sula bassana. Gannet.

Hydrobates pelagicus. Storm-petrel.

Oceanodroma leucorrhoa leucorrhoa. Fork-tailed
petrel.

Puffinus puffinus puffinus. Manx shearwater.

Fulmarus glacialis glacialis. Fulmar.

Streptopelia turtur turtur. Turtle-dove.

Hæmatopus ostralegus ostralegus. Oyster-
catcher.

Charadrius hiaticula hiaticula. Ringed plover.

Charadrius apricarius apricarius. British golden
plover.

Charadrius apricarius altifrons. Northern golden
plover.

Arenaria interpres interpres. Turnstone.

Crocethia alba. Sanderling.

Calidris alpina? subsp. Dunlin.

Calidris minuta. Little stint.

Calidris maritima maritima. Purple sandpiper.

Tringa ochropus. Green sandpiper.

Tringa totanus robusta. Iceland Redshank.

Tringa totanus totanus. Common Redshank.

Tringa nebularia. Greenshank.
Numenius arquata arquata. Curlew.
Numenius phæopus phæopus. Whimbrel.
Capella gallinago gallinago. Common snipe.
Sterna macrura. Arctic tern.
Larus argentatus argentatus. Herring-gull.
(Larus fuscus fuscus. Scandinavian lesser black-
  backed gull.)
Larus fuscus graellsii. British lesser black-backed
  gull.
Larus marinus. Great black-backed gull.
Rissa tridactyla tridactyla. Kittiwake.
Stercorarius pomarinus. Pomatorhine skua.
Alca torda. Razorbill.
Uria aalge? subsp. Guillemot.
Uria grylle grylle. Black guillemot.
Fratercula arctica grabæ. Puffin.

A few references have been made to the vegetation of the island. There is no heather, peat, or
peat-moss on North Rona, but it is possible to get
the dried turf to burn. For this purpose the inhabitants erected a number of stone cairns, called piles
on the map, which were probably used for the drying
of the turf. Driftwood on the island is very scarce,
and there is little sea-weed on the rocks. The only
record of the botany of the island is by R. M.
Barrington who recorded the following species on
North Rona:

Ranunculus flammula. Linn.
Ranunculus repens. Linn.
Cochlearia officinalis. Linn.

Cochlearia officinalis var. alpina.
Cerastium tetrandum. Curt.
Cerastium triviale. Link.
Stellaria media. With.
Sagina maritima. Don.
Sagina procumbens. Linn.
Montia fontana. Linn.
Trifolium repens. Linn.
Potentilla anserina. Linn.
Hydrocotyle vulgaris. Linn.
Ligusticum scoticum. Linn.
Angelica sylvestris. Linn.
Bellis perennis. Linn.
Matricaria inodora. Linn.
Leontodon autumnalis. Linn.
Armeria maritima. Willd.
Glaux maritima. Linn.
Plantago major. Linn.
Plantago coronopus. Linn.
Atriplex babingtonii. Woods.
Rumex acetosa. Linn.
Rumex acetosella. Linn.
Luzula (campestris, D.C.?)
Eleocharis palustris. R.Br.
Eriophorum angustifolium. Roth.
Carex vulgaris. With.
Aira praecox. Linn.
Holcus lanatus. Linn.
Poa pratensis. Linn.
Festuca rubra. Linn.
Nardus stricta. Linn.
Ophioglossum vulgatum. var. ambiguum. Linn.

Geology. The Geology of North Rona has now been worked out in great detail, only the broad outlines of which are given here. The island consists of hornblende gneiss intersected by pegmatite veins. Here the hornblende gneiss is of a very dark colour, and of moderately coarse texture. It consists essentially of hornblende which occupies a very large percentage of the rock, together with occasional crystals of augite. Both plagioclase and orthoclase felspars are present with a little quartz and oxides of iron. Much shattered garnets up to half an inch in diameter are common accessories. The pegmatite veins are of great size and consist of crystals of quartz and microcline felspar, which are often arranged in a graphic intergrowth. These veins are much more durable than the gneiss, and they thus play a large part in the scenic features of the island. The curious 'devil's scratches' at Leac na Sgrob are in reality nothing more than slickensides caused by differential land movement. Unfortunately, intense subsequent marine erosion has made it impossible to determine the exact cause for this movement. The presence of a deposit of cemented sand, suggesting a possible raised beach, and a few pieces of rock alien to the island, suggest that North Rona probably came under the influence of the quaternary ice, as was suggested by James Geikie. There is also an interesting storm beach on the west side of Fianuis which was noted and recorded by MacCulloch.

SULA SGEIR

As one looks west from North Rona on a fine day, one sees a small piece of land, a large sea rock, that for ever excites the imagination. For many years it was found impossible to visit it. Even the great MacCulloch, who found it impossible to land on, writes, 'To have visited Barra and Rona gives a claim to distinction scarcely less in their estimation than to have explored the sources of the Nile or the Niger'.

How best can one describe Sula Sgeir, this gannet rock, sitting in the midst of the Atlantic some eleven miles to the westward of Rona like a consort to it? 'What can be said of it', writes Muir, 'more than it is a high, horrent and nearly herbless strip of gneiss or other such adamantine matter, scarcely one-third of a mile in extent and so narrowed in many places that, in the winter time, the strepent wave must be evermore lashing over from side to side, and cutting up the whole mass into so many the merest of particles?'

The island of Sula Sgeir is in reality little more than a large sea rock. Situated in latitude 59° 6′ north, and longitude 6° 10′ west, it is half a mile long NNE.–SSW. with a maximum breadth of 200 yards. The highest point of 229 feet occurs at the extreme southern end, although that at the northern extremity must be almost of equal magnitude. Towards the centre the island is very narrow and low, being only some fifteen to twenty feet above the wave, so that on a rough night the sea breaks completely over this point, and divides the island into two similar portions.

It is, however, the southern portion of the island that holds one's interest, for it is here that the stone bothies and Muir's chapel are situated. On the widest part of the island are some five stone bothies of unique construction. They must measure some twelve feet long and eight feet across, while they are about six feet in height. They are all 'dry stone' built with slabs of rock of incredible size. They all possess a doorway, while some have another aperture as well, presumably a window. The walls of these buildings are in places nearly four feet thick and very substantially built. With the exception of one they are all complete with roofs, the huge flags of stone being built inwards towards the centre. Some of these bothies have a protecting wall built outside the doorway, while within the further half is raised by a small step. Around the walls, too, there is a solid stone bench.

There are altogether five bothies of a similar type, but no one knows for certain who was responsible for their construction, or when they were built. Such is the nature of the island that it is absolutely impossible to imagine that any one ever attempted to live there, and since as far back as 1594 there is no record of any one having inhabited the island, one feels that this assumption is fairly correct.

These buildings were all probably erected by men from the Lewis, who still go annually in September to snare the young gannets or 'gugas' as they are called. However, Muir claims—one does not know

Photo.

FIG. 16. SULA SGEIR FROM THE EAST

M.S.

on what authority—that the eastern of these bothies
is a chapel and he calls it Teampull Sula Sgeir. But so
far as it is possible to see this building is in every
respect the same as the others. As regards these
buildings one can only assume therefore that they
were built for the annual fowling; and for similar
purposes a wall and a small well were also erected
a little farther to the south of the island. For some
purpose, too, large flags of rock were set up on end
like monoliths. Some of these are at least five feet
in height.

The cliffs of Sula Sgeir are sheer, so that it is only
possible to land on one place on the island, namely
near Geodha Phuill Bhain, at the centre of the
eastern side; and even here there must indeed be
few days in the year when the sea is sufficiently calm
to allow an approach. All the cliffs are indented with
caves and geos, and in one place the sea has tunnelled
completely through the island. While the north and
the east of the island are clear of obstruction, the west
is surrounded by dangerous skerries, and a larger
skerry, Gralisgeir, lies off the extreme southern point.
The island is completely devoid of vegetation save
for a little sea pink and chickweed and similar plants
on the southern portion. A complete list of these
plants is given elsewhere.

There is really little more to be said of this desolate spot for, since no one has lived on it, it can have
but little history. The island has always been famous,
among those few who have ever been there, on
account of its wonderful bird life. So remunerative
is it in fact that men from Ness in the Lewis still go

G

there annually in September for the young birds, which on occasions fetch as much as one shilling each. One can see the results of their handiwork.

Quite apart from the actual buildings, there are to be found a few rusty iron implements—in one of the houses is an empty bottle and a large pot suspended by a chain from the roof, while a piece of old rotten sacking hangs in the doorway. Around are strewn the remains of dead birds. Among the clefts in the cliffs a few old oars and other pieces of wood are to be seen, while near the landing-place is some rusty chain, placed, no doubt, to facilitate the hazardous landing. Perhaps the next person to spend a night or two on the island, if any one might ever wish to do this, will also find in another house a few cans of water, some tinned food, and a spade, and wonder as to how they came there and who brought them.

Swinburne gives rather a pathetic story concerning a visit of the men of the Lewis. He writes: 'On one occasion now some years ago, a crew from Ness in the Lewis had their boat wrecked in landing on Sula Sgeir in the month of June, and lived on the island for several weeks, sustaining themselves on the flesh of birds. Captain Oliver, who commanded the Revenue cruiser *Prince of Wales*, visited Sula Sgeir in the month of August to look for the lost boat. He found a wreck on it, also an oar on end with an old pair of canvas trousers on it, and over the remains of a fire a pot containing birds' flesh; but there being no trace of the men, it was thought they must have been picked up by a passing vessel. Nothing more

Photo.   *M.S.*

FIG. 17. TEAMPULL SULA SGEIR

Photo.   *M.S.*

FIG. 18. THE SHEER CLIFFS
OF SULA SGEIR

was heard of them until the month of October following, when a Russian vessel on her homeward voyage met a Stornoway craft in the Orkneys, and informed the crew of the latter that they had taken the men off Sula Sgeir and landed them in Rona. Captain Oliver at once went to Rona, and found the crew consuming the last barrel of potatoes which the poor shepherd had. He took away the former, and left the latter sufficient provision for the winter.'

Like North Rona, Sula Sgeir also did not escape the ravages of the War, for we learn that 'On December 23rd the 2nd and 4th Battle Squadrons with the *Iron Duke* proceeded to sea to the westward of the Orkneys and carried out target practice at the Sulis-Ker rock, north of the Hebrides'.

NATURAL HISTORY

Sula Sgeir is, of course, chiefly known on account of its gannetry. Gurney estimated the number here at 8,000, and according to his reckoning there was no other gannetry in Scotland larger, with the exception of the island of Borreray, St. Kilda. There is no doubt, though, that the status of these birds in the various Scottish islands has changed somewhat since Gurney's census, and there is still much controversy at the present time concerning actual numbers. It is almost impossible to estimate the number of birds by gazing at the thousands nesting on the cliffs. The only way of obtaining a figure is from the records of the number of young gannets known to have been captured. In 1884 Harvie-

Brown informs us that 2,800 were taken in three consecutive days, while one learns that 2,500 were taken in 1898. Now 2,800 young gannets would have had 5,600 parents, and Gurney states that it is probable that 2,400 more gannets would have inaccessible nests. These figures therefore give 8,000. One learns that in 1915, 1,100 young birds were taken and sold at one shilling each, an advance of 3d. or 4d. on the usual price. Boats still go annually in September from Ness, and Mr. MacFarquhar states that about 2,000 young gannets are taken during the visit. Working on Gurney's methods this would give a total of about 6,500 adults. Mr. T. H. Harrisson made 'a rough long distance estimate at 9,000 adults on Sula Sgeir'. This figure, which can be little more than a guess, should not be relied upon. It is absolutely safe to say that, both by actual observation and by calculations based on the numbers of birds known to have been taken, Gurney's figures are well in excess of the present gannet population of Sula Sgeir. An interesting point concerning these gannets is that they nest only on the extreme southern portion of the island, an area not exceeding ten acres. A line has been drawn on the map giving the extreme northern limit. The gannets are thick south of this line and nest not only on the cliffs but also on the top in the open. The whole of the rock here is white with guano and the stench is indescribable. These birds are remarkably tame, it being easily possible to approach within a few feet of them.

Other very common birds on Sula Sgeir include

FIG. 19. THE SHEER CLIFFS OF SULA SGEIR

FIG. 20. 'SULA BASSANA', SULA SGEIR

the razorbill and guillemot. These are to be found everywhere on the cliffs and among the stones on the top of the island. In numbers they must exceed the gannets. Puffins, too, are very common, though their numbers would probably be much greater if there was more soil and turf for them to burrow in. Kittiwakes are present in very large numbers here and nest on ledges in the cliffs as on North Rona.

One of the most interesting features of bird life on Sula Sgeir is the life of the shag. This bird breeds here in the stone bothies, already mentioned. The only reason for the choice of this abode is probably on account of the shelter afforded. They are in complete occupation of these buildings, with the consequence that the floors are some six inches deep in straw and slime. The smell is, as might be expected, completely overpowering.

Other birds here include the fulmar, which as on Rona nests on the top of the island in the open, and shares the bothies with the shags. They are not, however, very numerous and probably do not exceed 150 pairs. The rock-pipit is also present, though it is difficult to estimate its numbers.

One who spends a night in or near the bothies of Sula Sgeir will without doubt be rudely awakened by cries and considerable commotion issuing from the walls of the buildings. So similar are the callings and nocturnal disturbances here, that one is at once reminded of nights spent among the ruins on North Rona. Unfortunately, time did not permit a thorough investigation. Though so far there is no record of

the Leach's fork tail petrel here, it is almost certain
that eventually it will be proved without a doubt
that Sula Sgeir is another breeding-place of this
interesting species. The flight is identical, as are all
the other characteristics, and there is really no reason
why this bird should not also breed here as well as
on North Rona and the Flannan Islands.

Vegetation is only very sparingly present on Sula
Sgeir, and only to be found at all around the buildings. Mr. C. P. Petch very kindly identified the
following species which were collected by the author
in the summer of 1932.

> Armeria maritima. Thrift.
> Matricaria inodora. Scentless margweed.
> Cochlearia officinalis. Scurvy grass.
> Atriplex (?) babingtonii. Orach.
> Stellaria media. Chickweed.

All the above specimens have been recorded both
from North Rona and from the Flannan Islands.
It is interesting to note that the northern half of the
island is entirely void of any vegetation, while the
amount of bird life on this part is also negligible
compared with the southern portion.

Geology. Like North Rona, Sula Sgeir consists of
hornblende gneiss. The gneiss, however, differs in
some respects from that of the former island. On
Sula Sgeir biotite is quite common as an accessory
mineral, while it was almost entirely absent from
Rona. The pegmatite veins here are all small and by
no means clearly defined, being nowhere comparable

Photo.   *M.S.*

FIG. 21. GANNETS ON SULA SGEIR

Photo.   *M.S.*

FIG. 22. GANNETS ON SRON NA LICE

with those of North Rona. If the quaternary ice reached that island, as seems probable, it is almost certain that it must also have reached Sula Sgeir only some eleven and a half miles to the west, and this is to some extent borne out by the presence on Sula Sgeir of small pieces of rock clearly alien to the island.

THE FLANNAN ISLANDS

. . . . .

We landed; and made fast the boat;
And climbed the track in single file,
Each wishing he were safe afloat,
On any sea, however far,
So be it far from Flannan Isle.

W. W. GIBSON.

THE weather had been bad, as it often is in wild
Loch Roag, and it was a whole week before
the voyage could be started. One morning,
however, in early August, as a small boat sailed into
Breasclete with a following wind, a man on the quay
regarded it with silent misgiving. Was this small
open boat with its single patched red sail to take
him across the open Atlantic? for the Flannans are
full twenty miles from Gallan Head and the Old
Hill. But others had done this voyage. Did not
the district superintendent travel to the light each
year in like manner, and did not the shepherds go
annually in this craft from Bernera to tend the sheep?
So he embarked, and the boat was pushed off, thus
commencing a voyage to the Flannans which was
destined to take thirteen and a half hours to cover
the twenty-five miles.

The Flannan Islands are a group of numerous
small islands and rocks in latitude 58° 17′ north
and longitude 7° 35′ west. So numerous and small
are these rocks and islands that it is difficult to
differentiate between them. There are, however,
principally seven islands which divide themselves

Photo.

M.S.

Fig. 23. EILEAN MOR FROM EILEAN TIGHE

naturally into three groups. A northern group, consisting of Eilean Mor and Eilean Tighe, a southern group: Soray, Sgeir Toman, and Sgeir Righinn, and a western group of Roareim and Eilean a Ghobha. These islands belong to the parish of Uig.

The following table gives their chief measurements.

MAXIMUM MEASUREMENTS

Isle.	N.–S. Ft.	E.–W. Ft.	Height. Ft.	Coast Miles.	Area Acres
Eilean Mor.	1,500	2,000	288	$1\frac{1}{4}$	39
Eilean Tighe	700	2,000	..	$1\frac{1}{8}$	18
Soray	400	1,000	..	$\frac{1}{2}$	8
Sgeir Toman	400	800	..	$\frac{1}{3}$	5
Sgeir Righinn	200	900	..	$\frac{1}{3}$	3
Roareim	700	800	150	$\frac{1}{2}$	7
Eilean a Ghobha	600	1,200	165	$\frac{1}{2}$	12

In comparison with their small area, all the islands are of remarkable height; in fact they appear from the sea as a series of immense cliffs topped by flat plateaux, and in every case landing is only possible in the very finest of weather, and even then is of extreme difficulty on account of the tide and Atlantic swell.

These islands are all uninhabited except for a light-house erected on Eilean Mor by the Commissioners of Northern Lighthouses in 1899. Little is known of these islands or of their history. There are the remains of two buildings on Eilean Mor. One of these is situated near the lighthouse and much resembles a large dog kennel. It is called Teampull

H

Beannachadh or Blessing House. It is some twelve
feet long and nine to ten feet broad externally, with
an internal height of about six feet to the top of the
sloping roof. The whole is 'dry stone' built, and the
roof of it is still more or less complete. There is a
very small and low doorway in the west end. It is
doubtful to whom this building belonged. 'Two
saints', says MacCulloch, 'seem to contest for the
honour of giving their name to the Flannan Islands;
St. Flannan was Bishop of Killaloe in 639, and he is
canonized in the Irish calendar, but St. Flann was the
son of Maol-duine, Abbot of Iona, who died in 890,
and who is to decide?' The obvious explanation of
the origin of this building, and the others on the
Flannans, is that they were erected to accommodate
the men from the Lewis who used to voyage there
annually to snare the birds. Unfortunately, however,
this matter cannot be proved either way.

Our early information concerning the island is due
to Martin, who tells us of the superstitions of the
men of the Lewis on their annual visits, and of the
various punctilios that they had to observe. 'To
the north-west of Gallan-head, and within six leagues
of it, lie the Flannan-Islands, which the seamen call
North-hunters; they are but small islands, and six in
number, and maintain about seventy sheep yearly.
The inhabitants of the adjacent lands of the Lewis,
having a right to these islands, visit them once every
summer, and there make a great purchase of fowls,
eggs, down, feathers, and quills. When they go to
sea, they have their boat well manned, and make
towards the islands with an east wind; but if before

FIG. 24. EILEAN MOR FROM THE EAST

FIG, 25. EILEAN MOR FROM THE SOUTH

or at the landing the wind turn westerly, they hoist
up sail, and steer directly home again. If any of their
crew is a novice, and not versed in the customs of the
place, he must be instructed perfectly in all the
punctilios observed here before landing; and to prevent inconveniences that they think may ensue upon
the transgression of the least nicety observed here,
every novice is always joined with another, that can
instruct him all the time of their fowling; so all the
boat's crew are matched in this manner. After their
landing, they fasten the boat to the sides of a rock,
and then fix a wooden ladder, by laying a stone at the
foot of it, to prevent its falling into the sea; and when
they are got up into the island, all of them uncover
their heads, and make a turn sun-ways round,
thanking God for their safety. The first instruction
given after landing, is not to ease nature in that place
where the boat lies, for that they reckon a crime of
the highest nature, and of dangerous consequence to
all their crew; for they have a great regard to that
very piece of the rock upon which they first set their
feet, after escaping the danger of the ocean.

'The biggest of these islands is called Island-More;
it has the ruins of a chappel dedicated to St. Flannan,
from whom the island derives its name. When they
are come within 20 paces of the altar, they all strip
themselves of their upper garments at once; and their
upper clothing being laid upon a stone, which stands
there on purpose for that use, all the crew pray three
times before they begin fowling: the first day they
say the first prayer, advancing towards the chappel
upon their knees; the second prayer is said as they

go round the chappel; the third is said hard by or at
the chappel; and this is their morning service. The
vespers are performed with the like number of
prayers. Another rule is that it is absolutely unlawful to kill a fowl with a stone, for that they reckon
a great barbarity, and directly contrary to antient
custom.

'It is also unlawful to kill a fowl before they ascend
by the ladder. It is absolutely unlawful to call the
island of St. Kilda (which lies thirty leagues south-
ward) by its proper Irish name Hirt, but only the
High Country. They must not so much as once name
the islands in which they are fowling, by the ordinary
name Flannan, but only the Country. There are
several other things that must not be called by their
common names: e.g. Visk, which in the language of
the natives signifies water, they call Burn: a rock,
which in their language is Creg, must here be called
Creuy, i.e. hard: Shore in their language expressed
by Claddach, must here be called Vah, i.e. a cave:
Sour in their language is expressed Gort, but must
here be called Gaire, i.e. sharp: Slippery, which is
expressed Bog, must be called Soft: and several
other things to this purpose. They account it also
unlawful to kill a fowl after evening prayers. There
is an antient custom, by which the crew is obliged
not to carry home any sheep-suet, let them kill ever
so many sheep in these islands. One of their principal
customs is not to steal or eat anything unknown to
their partner, else the transgressor (they say) will
certainly vomit it up; which they reckon as a just
judgement. When they have loaded their boat

Photo. C. Dick Peddie

FIG. 26. THE WEST LANDING,
EILEAN MOR

Photo. C. Dick Peddie.

FIG. 27. BEANNACHADH, EILEAN MOR

sufficiently with sheep, fowls, eggs, down, fish, &c.,
they make the best of their way homeward. It's
observed of the sheep of these islands that they are
exceedingly fat and have long horns.'

Towards the west of the island are some further
ruins, but it is now impossible to tell their original
shape and form. They are known as Bothien Clann
Igphail (the bothies of MacPhail's sons), but this
information unfortunately conveys little.

On Eilean Tighe (the island of the house) there
are also ruins to be found. At the further end of the
large geo on the west is a collection of stones
arranged in an oval to round formation with a
diameter of some eleven feet. The walls now stand
about three and a half feet high and are three feet
thick. The remains of a small door on the east side
are still to be seen. There is also another structure at
the extreme east end of the island; this is in every
way similar to the former, though only some seven
and a half feet across. It seems strange that no one
has ever mentioned these buildings on Eilean Tighe
before, when the name is so suggestive.

There is really very little else of interest in the
Flannan Islands. The islands are all high and very
steep, and like North Rona they are often covered in
mist. The western group is similar to the southern
group, though here the passage between the islands
is completely blocked with small skerries against
which the sea breaks incessantly. However, one of
the best sights in these isles is the view of Brona
Cleit from Roareim. Brona Cleit is a needle-shaped
stack some hundred feet high, and stands like a

miniature Stac an Armin as a sentinel on this forbidding coast.

One cannot pass on without mentioning a few words about the lighthouse. This lighthouse is situated on the top of Eilean Mor at the north-east end. It consists of a low white tower and lantern, surrounded by a low white building which is the store and living quarters of the keepers. The landing on Eilean Mor must at one time have been almost impossible, but now two landing-places have been made. At each is a large crane to haul up the oil and stores, and in bad weather even the men themselves have to be taken on and off in this manner. These 'landings' are so placed that it is possible to land on the island at one of them on practically any day of the year. From each 'landing' to the lighthouse there is a small rail track on which runs a trolley operated by a cable wound up by steam from the lighthouse. This is in every way necessary to take the oil and stores up the steep slope from the 'landing' to the light.

Whether people no longer observe the punctilios of Martin, or for what other reason no one knows, but the Flannans have always been associated with disaster. The very islands look forbidding. North Rona is green, fertile, and happy, an island that wants to be visited; Sula Sgeir, though inhospitable, has its charm. No one can fail to be fascinated by St. Kilda, but the Flannans induce a feeling of awe and despondency. Their towering black cliffs are ever objects of fear and terror. Every one has now heard of the tragedy of the Flannans, of 'the three men alive on Flannan Isle, who thought on three men dead'.

Photo.   *C. E. Cadger.*

FIG. 28. BOTHIEN CLANN IGPHAIL

Photo.   *M.S.*

FIG. 29. RUINS, EILEAN TIGHE

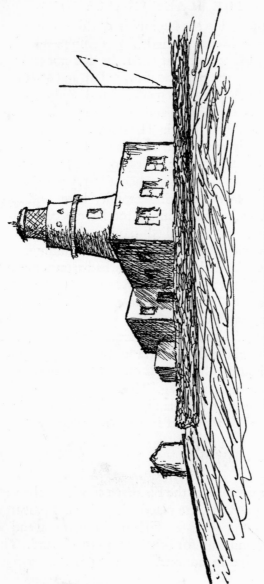

Fig. 30. LIGHTHOUSE, EILEAN MOR

(W. L. ROOTS)

It happened in the beginning of this century, soon after the light was erected, that a ship passed in the night and reported that the light was not showing. After a time the relief boat turned up and after much difficulty a landing was made. But though the whole island was searched up and down no one of the three keepers was ever found. The mystery has never been satisfactorily explained, and the only possible solution is that they were all on one of the 'landings' lashing down the crane, when a heavy sea came on, as they do with amazing rapidity here, and swept them all off. Other troubles too have occurred here, for one man was killed having fallen from the tower, while others have been lost in landing.

These islands have indeed a bad name, but now the conditions there are much improved. The lighthouse is installed with wireless telephone, and twice every twenty-four hours the keepers have to call up the Butt of Lewis. There are four keepers of the Flannan light and one extra keeper, three are always on the island, while one is off at the shore station at Breasclete in Loch Roag. The men serve two months continuously on the island, and then have one month ashore, while the relief is made monthly by the *Pole Star*.

NATURAL HISTORY

The mammals of the Flannans consist of the sheep that, as on Rona, are placed there for the pasturage. They belong to three farmers in Bernera and are changed annually for others from that island. They are fifty-five in number, and such is the supposed

value of the pasturage that a few are kept on nearly all
the islands. The number on each island is as under:

Eilean Mor	. 21	Sgeir Toman .	3
Eilean Tighe	. 12	Roareim . .	3
Soray	. . 8	Eilean a Ghobha	8

Like North Rona and Sula Sgeir, the Flannans are
also a favourite haunt of *Halichoerus grypus*, the grey
seal, though it is doubtful if it breeds here.

Early keepers on Eilean Mor unfortunately had
the idea of keeping rabbits on the island, with the
consequence that the whole island is now teeming
with these skinny wretches. It is a great pity that
people will put these vermin on small islands such
as this. The rabbits are of no use to any one and
multiply with such rapidity that in a few years the
islands are completely overrun. In the case of Eilean
Mor the grazing is now completely spoiled, although
this island used to have the most luxuriant vegetation of any. Luckily, both North Rona and St. Kilda
have so far escaped this pest. There are no mice or
rats on the Flannans.

Among the birds, the Leach's fork tail petrel is by
far the most important. This unique species breeds
here in large numbers in holes in the turf near the
flagstaff on Eilean Mor. The puffin is very common
on the Flannans, as is also the fulmar, shag, and
kittiwake. The following list of resident and migratory birds is taken from Eagle Clarke who spent a
fortnight on Eilean Mor in 1904.

Corvus corax. Raven.
Corvus cornix. Grey Crow.

Corvus frugilegus. Rook.
Corvus monedula. Jackdaw.
Sternus vulgaris. Starling.
Fringilla cœlebs. Chaffinch.
Fringilla montifringilla. Brambling.
Chloris chloris. Greenfinch.
(Spinus spinus. Siskin.)
Acanthis cannabina. Linnet.
Acanthis flavirostris. Twite.
Acanthis linaria. Mealy Redpoll.
Acanthis rostrata. Greater Redpoll.
Loxia curvirostra. Crossbill.
Loxia bifasciata. Two-Barred Crossbill.
Emberiza citrinella. Yellow Bunting.
Emberiza schœniclus. Reed-Bunting.
Calcarius lapponicus. Lapland Bunting.
Plectrophenax nivalis. Snow-Bunting.
Zonotrichia albicollis. White-Throated Spar-
row.
Alauda arvensis. Skylark.
Alauda cinerea. Asiatic Skylark.
Calandrella brachydactyla. Short-Toed Lark.
Motacilla alba. White Wagtail.
(Motacilla thunbergi. Grey-Headed Wagtail.)
Motacilla lugubris. Pied Wagtail.
Anthus pratensis. Meadow-Pipit.
Anthus obscurus. Rock-Pipit.
Anthus trivialis. Tree-Pipit.
Lanius collurio. Red-Backed Shrike.
Regulus regulus. Goldcrest.
Sylvia sylvia. Common Whitethroat.
Sylvia curruca. Lesser Whitethroat.

Sylvia atricapilla. Blackcap.
Sylvia borin. Garden-Warbler.
Phylloscopus trochilus. Willow-Warbler.
Acrocephalus schœnobænus. Sedge-Warbler.
Turdus musicus. Song-Thrush.
Turdus iliacus. Redwing.
Turdus pilaris. Fieldfare.
Turdus merula. Blackbird.
Turdus torquatus. Ring-Ouzel.
Erithacus rubecula. Redbreast.
Ruticilla phœnicurus. Redstart.
Ruticilla titys. Black Redstart.
Saxicola œnanthe. Wheatear.
Pratincola rubetra. Whinchat.
Pratincola rubicola. Stonechat.
Troglodytes troglodytes. Wren.
Muscicapa grisola. Spotted Flycatcher.
Muscicapa atricapilla. Pied Flycatcher.
Hirundo rustica. Swallow.
Chelidon urbica. House-Martin.
Cotile riparia. Sand-Martin.
Cypselus apus. Swift.
Cuculus canorus. Cuckoo.
Asio accipitrinus. Short-Eared Owl.
Nyctea nyctea. Snowy Owl.
Falco peregrinus. Peregrine Falcon.
Falco æsalon. Merlin.
Falco candicans. Greenland Falcon.
Falco islandus. Iceland Falcon.
Falco tinnunculus. Kestrel.
Phalacrocorax carbo. Cormorant.
Phalacrocorax graculus. Shag.

Sula bassana. Gannet.
Ardea cinerea. Heron.
Anser sp. (?) 'Grey Geese.'
Branta bernicla. Brent Goose.
Branta leucopsis. Bernacle Goose.
Nettion crecca. Teal.
Mergus serrator. Merganser.
Somateria mollissima. Eider Duck.
Columba palumbus. Ring-Dove.
Turtur turtur. Turtle Dove.
Crex crex. Corn-Crake.
Gallinula chloropus. Waterhen.
Glareola pratincola. Pratincole.
(Squatarola helvetica. Grey Plover.)
Ægialitis hiaticola. Ringed Plover.
Eudromias morinellus. Dotterel.
Charadrius pluvialis. Golded Plover.
Vanellus vanellus. Lapwing.
Strepsilas interpres. Turnstone.
Hæmatopus ostralegus. Oyster-Catcher.
Phalaropus fulicarius. Grey Phalarope.
Scolopax rusticula. Woodcock.
Gallinago gallinago. Common Snipe.
Gallinago gallinula. Jack Snipe.
Tringa alpina. Dunlin.
Tringa striata. Purple Sandpiper.
Tringa canutus. Knot.
Calidris arenaria. Sanderling.
Totanus calidris. Redshank.
Numenius arquata. Curlew.
Numenius phæopus. Whimbrel.
Sterna macrura. Arctic Tern.

Larus ridibundus. Black-Headed Gull.
Larus marinus. Great Black-Backed Gull.
Larus fuscus. Lesser Black-Backed Gull.
Larus argentatus. Herring Gull.
Rissa tridactyla. Kittiwake.
Stercorarius crepidatus. Arctic Skua.
Alca torda. Razorbill.
Uria triole. Common Guillemot.
Cepphus grylle. Black Guillemot.
Alle alle. Little Auk.
Fratercula arctica. Puffin.
Procellaria pelagica. Storm Petrel.
Oceanodroma leucorrhoa. Fork-tailed Petrel.
Fulmarus glacialis. Fulmar.
Puffinis anglorum. Manx Shearwater.
Puffinis gravis. Great Shearwater.
Podicipes auritus. Slavonian Grebe.

Professor T. Hudson Beare has identified the
following eleven species of *Coleoptera* collected by
Eagle Clarke:

Carabus catenulatus. Scop.
Pterostichus niger. Schal.
Nebria brevicollis. F.
Calathus cisteloides. Pz.
Notiophilus biguttatus. F.
Calathus melanocephalus. L.
Trechus obtusus. Er.
Ocypus ater. Gr.
Philonthus varius. Gyll.
Aphodius rufipes. L.
Choleva grandicollis. Er.

William Evans records two species of Spiders from Eilean Mor, namely,

Trochosa terricola. Thor.
Drassus troglodytes. C.L.K.

Two slugs, *Arion ater*, and *Limax agrestis*, were recorded by Eagle Clarke.

From a collection by Eagle Clarke on Eilean Mor, the following thirty-five species of *Diptera* were identified by Percy H. Grimshaw:

Sciara spp.
Scatopse notata. L.
Chironomidæ.
Pericoma sp.
Tipula? confusa, V. d. Wlp.
Tipula paludosa. Mg.
Sympycnus annulipes. Mg.
Syrphus corollæ. F.
Syrphus luniger. Mg.
Cynomyia mortuorum. L.
Musca domestica. L.
Calliphora erythrocephala. Mg.
Euphoria cornicina. F.
Spilogaster duplicata. Mg.
Spilogaster sp.
Hydrotæa irritans. Fln.
Anthomyia sulciventris. Ztt.
Phorbia florilega. Ztt.
Phorbia sp.
Homalomyia canicularis. L.
Scatophaga stercoraria. L.
Scatophaga litorea. Fln.

Scatophaga squalida. Mg.
Cœlopa (? or Fucomyia) spp.
Blepharoptera modesta. Mg.
Scatella sibilans. Hal.
Scatella stagnalis. Hal.
Drosophila graminum. Fln.
Agromyza sp.
Ceratomyza denticornis. Panz.
Chromatomyia affinis. Mg.
Borborus geniculatus. Mcq.
Limosina crassimana. Hal.
Ornithomyia avicularia. L.

Our knowledge of the botany of the Flannan
Islands is due to James W. H. Trail who identified
the following thirteen species from Eilean Mor:

Ranunculus acris. L.
Cochlearia officinalis. L.
Silene maritima. With.
Stellaria media. L.
Cerastium triviale. Link.
Sagina procumbens. L. with Puccina arenariæ.
  Schum.
Matricaria inodora. L.
Glaux maritima. L.
Armeria maritima. L.
Plantago maritima. L.
Plantago coronopus. L.
Atriplex babingtonii. Woods.
Holcus lanatus. L.

Geology. The Flannan Islands all consist of hornblende gneiss intersected by pegmatite veins. This

gneiss differs somewhat from that of North Rona and Sula Sgeir in that biotite is a much more common constituent. While the character of the gneiss remains constant, the pegmatite veins vary greatly when traced from one island to another. On Eilean Mor the pegmatite exhibits a very marked graphic structure, the felspar here being white. Crystals of biotite are common accessories. On the other islands, however, the pegmatite resembles more that of North Rona. A few dykes of later age occur in these islands. Mr. W. J. MacCallien has recorded a small tholeiitic dyke on Eilean Mor, while on Eilean a Ghobha the author has found a much weathered and highly felspathic dyke, of apparently trachytic character. On the top of Roareim is to be found a deposit of cemented sand much resembling that on North Rona and it is possible that this may be a raised beach. In view of this, and the fact that on most of the islands there are small pieces of alien rock, one of which closely resembles a piece of fine-grained Torridon sandstone, while a few others are as yet unidentified, suggest that these islands were subjected to the influence of the quaternary ice. This indeed seems probable, as it is generally assumed that the Lewis and the Harris, only twenty miles distant, were swamped during this period.

APPENDIX I

DESCRIPTION OF THE WESTERN ISLES OF SCOTLAND CALLED HYBRIDES

By MR. DONALD MONRO

High Dean of the Isles,

Who travelled through the most of them
In the Year 1594

193. SEVEN HALEY ISLES. First, furth 50 myle in the Occident seas from the coste of the parochin Vye in Lewis, towarts the west northwest, lyes the seven iles of Flanayn, claid with girth, and Haley isles, verey natural gressing within thir saids iles; infinit wyld scheipe therein, quhilk na man knawes to quhom the said sheipe apperteines within them that lives this day of the countrymen; bot M'Cloyd of the Lewis, at certaine tymes in the zeir, sendis men in, and huntis and slayis maney of thir sheipe. The flesche of thir sheipe cannot be eaten be honest men for fatnesse, for ther is na flesche on them, bot all quhyte lyke talloune, and it is verey wyld gusted lykways. The saids iles are nouder manurit nor inhabit, bot full of grein high hills, full of wyld sheipe in the seven iles forsaid, quhilk may not be outrune. They perteine to M'Cloyd of the Lewis.

208. RONAY. Towards the north northeist from Lewis, three score myles of sea, lyes ane little ile callit Ronay, laiche maine lande, inhabit and manurit be simple people, scant of ony religione. This ile is uther haffe myle lange, and haffe myle braide;

K

aboundance of corne growes on it by delving onlie, aboundance of clover gerse for sheipe. Ther is an certain number of ky and sheipe ordainit for this ile be thir awin ald right, extending to sa maney as may be sustainit upon the said gerssing, and the countrey is so fertill of gerssing, that the superexcrescens of the said ky and scheipe baith feidis them in flesche, and als payes ther dewties with the samen for the maist pairt. Within this ile there is sic faire whyte beir meil made like flour, and quhen they slay ther sheipe, they slay them belly flaught, and stuffes ther skins fresche of the bear meil, and send their dewties be a servant of M'Cloyd of Lewis, with certain reistit muttan, and mony reistit foulis. Within this ile is ane chapell, callit St. Ronay's chapell, unto quhilk chapell, as the anceints of the country alledges, they leave an spaid and ane shuil, quhen any man dies, and upon the morrow findes the place of the grave markit with an spaid, as they alledge. In this ile they use to take maney quhailes and uthers grate fisches.

209. SUILSKERAY. Be sexteen myle of sea to this ile, towards the west, lyes ane ile callit Suilskeray, ane myle lang, without grasse or hedder, with highe blacke craigs, and black fouge thereupon part of them. This ile is full of wylde foulis, and quhen foulis hes ther birdes, men out of the parochin of Nesse in Lewis use to sail ther, and to stay ther seven or aught dayes, and to fetch hame with them their boitt full of dray wild foulis, with wyld foulis fedders. In this ile ther haunts ane kynd of foule

callit colk, little less nor a guise, quha comes in the
ver to the land to lay hir eggis, and to clecke hir
birds quhill she bring them to perfytness, and at that
time her fleiche of fedderis falleth of her all hailly,
and she sayles to the mayne sea againe, and comes
never to land quhyll the zeir end againe, and then she
comes with her new fleiche of fedderis. This fleiche
that she leaves zeirly upon her nest hes nae pens in
the fedderis, nor nae kind of hard thinge in them
that may be felt or graipit, bot utter fyne downes.

APPENDIX II

IMPORTANT EVENTS IN THE HISTORY OF THE ISLANDS OF NORTH RONA AND SULA SGEIR

Year	Event	Authority
8th or 9th cent.	St. Ronan leaves Eorrapidth and builds east end of chapel on Rona	Muir
?	The building of the supposed Teampull Sula Sgeir by an unknown hermit	Muir
10th or 11th cent.	West end of chapel on Rona built	Muir
pre 1260	Teampull nam Manach built, and destroyed about this year	Muir
1594	Visit of Dean Monro	Monro
?	Visit of Sir Robert Sibbald	Sibbald
1685	Plague of rats about this year; island subsequently re-populated.	Martin
pre 1703	Visit of Daniel Morison	Martin
1777	John Ogilvie's poem published	Ogilvie
1812	Voyage of the *Fortunée*. One family of six on Rona	MacCulloch
1814	MacCulloch visited Rona about this year	MacCulloch
1844	Evacuation of North Rona. Donald MacLeod 'King of Rona'	Muir
1850	Sir James Matheson offered Rona about this year gratis to the government as a penal settlement. The offer was refused.	*Ordnance Gazette of Scotland*
1852	Capt. Burnaby visited Rona on 3 February	Muir

Year	Event	Authority
1857	Muir visited North Rona	Muir
1860	Muir again visited North Rona and Sula Sgeir in July	Muir
1883	Visit to North Rona and Sula Sgeir of John Swinburne, on 19 June	Swinburne
1885	Deaths of Malcolm MacLeod and M. McKay on Rona, 18 February	Harvie-Brown
1885	Visit to Rona of Barrington, Harvie-Brown and Barclay, 29 June to 1 July	Harvie-Brown and Buckley
1887	Visit of Harvie-Brown and Heddle to Rona and Sula Sgeir	Harvie-Brown
1907	Visit of the Duchess of Bedford	Bedford
1910	The Duchess of Bedford visited Rona on 19 and 25 August	Bedford
1914(?)	H.M.S. *Sappho* visited North Rona on 23 August	Jellicoe
1915(?)	Target practice at Sula Sgeir	Jellicoe
1924	Visit to North Rona of the Commissioners of Historical Monuments.	Commiss. Hist. Mon.
1927	J. Wilson Dougal visited North Rona on 29 July	Dougal
1930	Visit of D. M. Reid and the author to North Rona, 31 July to 4 August	
1931	Visit of T. H. Harrisson and the author to North Rona, 28 August to 3 September	
1932	Visit of the author to Sula Sgeir, 23 to 24 July	

BIBLIOGRAPHY

NORTH RONA AND SULA SGEIR

BARRINGTON, R. M. 'Plants observed on North Rona July 1, 1886' in Harvie-Brown's 'Further Notes on North Rona'. *Proceedings of the Royal Physical Society of Edinburgh*, vol. ix, Pt. 1, 1885, p. 289.

BEDFORD, The Duchess of. 'On visits paid to the island of North Rona.' *Annals of Scottish Natural History*, 1910, pp. 212–14.

'Spring bird notes from various Scottish islands.' *Annals of Scottish Natural History*, 1914, pp. 179–80.

CLYNE, Robert. 'Movements of the Gannet as observed at the Butt of Lewis.' *Scottish Naturalist*, 1916, p. 57.

COMMISSION ON ANCIENT AND HISTORICAL MONUMENTS AND CONSTRUCTIONS OF SCOTLAND, ROYAL. 9. *Church, etc., North Rona.* 4°. Edin. 1928, pp. 3–4, vii.

DOUGAL, J. Wilson. 'A lonely island.' *Weekly Scotsman*, 14 July 1928.

'Crossbills in the Outer Isles'. *Scottish Naturalist*, 1927, p. 160.

GEIKIE, James. *The Great Ice Age*, 3rd edit. 8°. Lond. 1894, p. 157.

GURNEY, J. H. *The Gannet.* 8°. Lond. 1913, pp. 150–4.

HARRISON, T. H. 'Resident and migratory birds of North Rona, the remotest Scottish Island.' *The Ibis*, July 1932, pp. 441–57.

'The number of the Grey Seal, Halichoerus grypus, on St. Kilda and North Rona.' *Journal of Animal Ecology*, vol. i, No. 1, May 1932, p. 83.

'Counts of Gannets (Sula bassana) in Scottish Islands'. *Journal of Animal Ecology*, vol. ii, No. 1, May 1933, p. 116.

HARVIE-BROWN, J. A. 'Further Notes on North Rona.' *Proceedings of the Royal Physical Society of Edinburgh*, vol. ix, Pt. 1, 1885, pp. 284–98.

'The Fulmar.' *Scottish Naturalist*, 1912, pp. 126–7.

HARVIE-BROWN, J. A., and BUCKLEY, T. E. *A vertebrate fauna of the Outer Hebrides.* 8°. Edin. 1888, pp. xxxv–liv.

HEDDLE, M. F. 'On the geological features of the Outer Hebrides.' In Harvie-Brown's *Vertebrate Fauna, &c.,* pp. 229–30.

The Mineralogy of Scotland. 8°. Edin. 1901.

JELLICOE, Viscount. *The Grand Fleet*, 1914–16. 8°. Lond. 1919, pp. 107 and 183.

MARTIN, Martin. *A Description of the Western Islands of Scotland, &c.* 8°. Lond. 1716, pp. 19–26.

MONRO, Donald. *Description of the Western Isles of Scotland.* Reprinted in *Miscellanea Scotica.* 8°. Glasg. 1818, vol. ii, pp. 152–3.

MUIR, T. S. *Characteristics of Old Church Architecture.* 4°. Edin. 1861, pp. 189–206.

Incholm, Aberdour, N. Rona, Sula Sgeir: (a sketch), 1872.

Transactions of the Society of Antiquaries of Scotland, vol. v, 1890, p. 245.

Ecclesiological Notes on some of the Islands of Scotland. 8°. Edin. 1885, pp. 80–99.

MACCULLOCH, John. *A Description of the Western Islands of Scotland.* 8°. Lond. 1819, vol. i, pp. 204–11.

The Highlands and Western Isles of Scotland. 8°. Lond. 1824, vol. iii, pp. 301–22.

Transactions of the Geological Society of London, 1814, p. 391.

OGILVIE, John. *Rona, a poem in seven books.* 4°. Lond. 1777.

REID, D. M. 'Our loneliest isle.' *Cornhill Magazine,* Sept. 1931, pp. 341–8.

SIBBALD, Sir Robert. 'An account of Hirta and Rona', &c. Printed in Pinkerton's *Gen. Coll. voyages & travels,* vol. iii, p. 730. 4°. Lond. 1809.

STEWART, Malcolm. 'Notes on the Geology of North Rona.' *Geological Magazine,* April 1932, pp. 179–85.

'Notes on the Geology of Sula Sgeir and the Flannan Islands.' *Geological Magazine,* March 1933, pp. 110–16.

SWINBURNE, John. 'Notes on the islands of Sula Sgeir or North Barra and North Rona, with a list of the birds inhabiting them.' *Proceedings of the Royal Physical Society of Edinburgh,* vol. viii, Pt. 1, 1883, pp. 51–67.

THE FLANNAN ISLANDS

BEARE, T. Hudson. 'Notes on some Coleoptera from the Flannan Islands.' *Annals of Scottish Natural History*, 1905, pp. 20–2.

COMMISSION ON ANCIENT AND HISTORICAL MONUMENTS AND CONSTRUCTIONS OF SCOTLAND, ROYAL. 105. *Chapel, Flannain Isles*, and 106. *Bothies of the Clan MacPhail.* 4°. Edin. 1928, p. 30.

EAGLE CLARKE, W. 'The Birds of the Flannan Islands; Outer Hebrides.' *Annals of Scottish Natural History*, 1905, pp. 8–19 and 80–6.
Studies in Bird Migration. 8°. Lond. 1912, vol. ii, pp. 250–85.

EVANS, William. 'Spiders from the Flannan Isles.' *Annals of Scottish Natural History*, 1905, p. 120.

GIBSON, W. J. 'A Visit to the Seven Hunters.' *Chambers Journal*, 1899, pp. 795–8.

GIBSON, W. W. 'Flannan Isle.' A poem in *Fires.* 8°. Lond. 1915, pp. 44–7.

GRIMSHAW, Percy H. 'On the Diptera of the Flannan Islands.' *Annals of Scottish Natural History*, 1905, pp. 218–20.

HARVIE-BROWN, J. A. 'The Fulmar.' *Scottish Naturalist*, 1912, pp. 127–8.

HARVIE-BROWN, J. A., and BUCKLEY, T. E. *A Vertebrate Fauna of the Outer Hebrides.* 8°. Edin. 1888, pp. xxiii–xxxiv.

MARTIN, Martin. *A Description of the Western Islands of Scotland, &c.* 8°. Lond. 1716, pp. 15–19.

MONRO, Donald. *Description of the Western Isles of Scotland.* Reprinted in *Miscellanea Scotica.* 8°. Glasg. 1818, vol. ii, p. 148.

MUIR, T. S. *Characteristics of Old Church Architecture.* 4°. Edin. 1861, pp. 178–82.
Ecclesiological Notes on some of the Islands of Scotland. 8°. Edin. 1885, pp. 58–60.

MACCALLIEN, William J. 'Rocks from the Flannan Islands'. *Transactions of the Geological Society of Glasgow*, vol. xviii, Pt. 3, 1928–31, p. 625.

'Geology of the Flannan Islands'. *Geological Magazine.* June 1933, p. 288.

MACCULLOCH, John. *A Description of the Western Islands of Scotland.* 8°. Lond. 1819, vol. i, pp. 198–203.
The Highlands and Western Isles of Scotland. 8°. Lond. 1824, vol. iii, pp. 198–207.

STEWART, Malcolm. 'Notes on the Geology of Sula Sgeir and the Flannan Islands.' *Geological Magazine,* March 1933, pp. 110–16.

TRAIL, James W. H. 'The Plants of the Flannan Islands.' *Annals of Scottish Natural History,* 1905, p. 187.

PRINTED IN
GREAT BRITAIN
AT THE
UNIVERSITY PRESS
OXFORD
BY
JOHN JOHNSON
PRINTER
TO THE
UNIVERSITY